How to Escape a Burning House

poems by

Eileen Lawrence

Finishing Line Press
Georgetown, Kentucky

How to Escape a Burning House

Copyright © 2025 by Eileen Lawrence
ISBN 979-8-89990-170-6 First Edition
All rights reserved under International and Pan-American Copyright Conventions. No part of this book may be reproduced in any manner whatsoever without written permission from the publisher, except in the case of brief quotations embodied in critical articles and reviews.

Publisher: Leah Huete de Maines
Editor: Christen Kincaid
Cover Art: Eileen Lawrence
Author Photo: Eileen Lawrence
Cover Design: Elizabeth Maines McCleavy

Order online: www.finishinglinepress.com
also available on amazon.com

Author inquiries and mail orders:
Finishing Line Press
PO Box 1626
Georgetown, Kentucky 40324
USA

Contents

Unfurled 1
Moving Out 2
Premonition 4
Divorce Litany 5
The Secret I Keep From Myself 7
Time Travel 8
Astrophysics at the Dinner Table 9
You Ask Me 10
Tightrope 11
Where to Cry 13
Question 41, New Patient Questionnaire 14
Ophidiophobia 15
The Beginning 17
Light/Dark 18
The Weaver 19
Fargo, November 20
My Private Music 21
The Night Before My Husband Hid the Gun 22
Flight 23
The Big Red Grill 24
My (Un)Broken Home 26
For My Younger Child 27
I Am the Hero In My Story and the Villain In His ... 28
Kintsugi: A Family Portrait 29
How to Escape a Burning House 31
Reunion 32
I Know This Is a Bad Time 33
The Playground 34
Postmortem 36
He Felt Like Home 37

For all of the mothers who feel alone.

*I thought I was alone who suffered.
I went on top of the house,
And found every house on fire.*

—Baba Sheikh Farid

Unfurled

I imagine a butterfly feels this way
when it first emerges from its chrysalis
wings wet, trusting the air to hold it aloft,
or when it dreams caterpillar dreams
and wakes up, winged, and far from the ground.

I was stuck on the ground too, once
held there by invisible forces,
and now I dance in the breeze
weightless and full of wonder.
I don't know what I did
to deserve this joy and beauty.

(Sometimes I lose my balance, forgetting
that I am no longer a caterpillar,
that my wings are strong,
that I live on nectar instead of bitter leaves.
The past can be a heavy thing.)

Do butterflies also wonder
what they did to deserve such a glorious life?
Do they pity the caterpillars?
Or do the butterflies dance for them—
a dance of hope and joy
and the promise of better things to come?

Moving Out

I flew home from Chicago on Sunday,
heart in my throat, my flight delayed.
On Saturday, we'd agreed that I'd have a week
to move out of our house.

When I got home, our children raged at me.
I blistered under their anger.
You'd told them it was my fault
before you drove away.

I held them, cried with them, reassured them,
promised new pets in our new apartment.
I stayed in their bedroom that night until they fell asleep,
wondering if we'd survive this.

Somehow I got them to school the next morning.
For three hours a day the next five days
(while our children sat at school, broken and angry),
I unstitched the fabric of our marriage.

I packed my clothes and my favorite books,
my grandmother's paintings,
half of our children's clothes,
half of their toys.

(Our pictures and papers were the hardest to disentangle
but I didn't have time to brood
—mine, yours, mine, yours, mine, yours—
that was the only time I cried.)

I rented a storage space,
found a furnished apartment.
Crammed clothes and toys into grocery bags
when I ran out of boxes.

(The gun I'd hidden with a friend
before I told you I was leaving
—just in case—
I placed back into its safe, unloaded.)

Every afternoon I suspended my hasty packing
to sit with our children, hold them,
cry with them, read to them,
rock with them, sing to them.

Each day was a little easier—
maybe they realized they weren't losing me,
maybe they saw my back straightening,
felt the lifting of the weight that had settled on my shoulders.

By Friday afternoon,
they were excited to see their new apartment.
The three of us ate ice cream in our new kitchen,
played hide-and-seek, squealing, in the hallways.

My last day in our house, Saturday,
was a sunny day, warm for Fargo in April.
I knew I'd have to leave my children in a few hours
for longer than I'd ever been away from them.

So we walked around our neighborhood.
They wore their colorful cloth butterfly wings.
We danced and twirled and laughed,
warming ourselves in the sunlight.

Premonition

The wind against my window warns of a storm,
as my children murmur,
foreboding creeping into their dreams.
My oldest cries out
as he rolls over to escape his fear.

I lie awake, listening
to the wind rattling the window
and the breathing of the man next to me,
my children's father.

I know the wind is not what's blown between us,
rattling our bond.
I know what fear haunts my children's dreams.
I know it's not the storm cracking their foundation,
but my own will.

Divorce Litany

twenty-two years together
sixteen and a half years of marriage
four degrees—two each
ten moves, three states
seventeen jobs (fourteen for me)
one career sidetracked—
two children
four cats, one dog
one major depressive disorder
three antidepressant prescriptions

He asks, "Do you love me?'
and I pause,
say "no."
It is Fargo in February,
everything dead under once pristine
snow now fouled with exhaust, dirt, smoke

Thus began
the renegotiation of our relationship,
and by "renegotiation" I mean
Pangea renegotiating herself into separate
continents,
shifting of tectonic plates

> *If you leave me, only your parents and your sister will love you.*

lava gushing from deep wounds

> *How can you do this to me? How can you do this to our children?*

earthquakes splitting solid ground

> *You can leave this house right now. You will never see our children again.*

species vanished, fossilized

Mom, why did you divorce us?

islands surging sharply upward,

                      gasping for air

The Secret I Keep From Myself

Your mother didn't tell you
(maybe she didn't know)
that sometimes sex between a husband and wife is beautiful and lifegiving
and sometimes it is
      your body turned away from his as you feign sleep
      his large hand moving fabric out of his way so he can push himself
      into you
           without first whispering words of love
           or gently caressing your skin
each thrust a violation
a breaking
of your marriage vows
and you cannot say No or Stop because that means
he is really doing this to you
and you are allowing it

you wait for it to be over

Then it is over and he turns away.
Liquid pools on your exposed thighs and
tears spill into your pillow and
you taste blood from where you bit the inside of your cheek

you are afraid to move because if you move
you will have to admit that he took this
from you and you can't face that,
so you stay in your bed, stay
in your marriage
because no one told you that rape
does not have to mean a knife or a gun or a back alley or threats or force
rape can be your husband in your marriage
bed where you made children together, rape can be
silent submission.

That is why
you keep this secret from yourself—
so it won't
break you.

Time Travel

I slip into bed between
the two of them
curve my body around hers
(my back solid against him).
She can't feel my arm resting against
her silently shuddering ribcage,
can't feel my breath on her neck
or hear what I whisper in her ear:
you are stronger than you know,
there are better days coming.
But maybe she draws something from me:
strength to rest, to make plans,
courage, hope,
a knowing
that what seems impossible
is at her fingertips.
She can't hear me,
but I know the path
she will travel, I know
how she starves for a giving touch.
So I wrap my arms around her,
and hold her close.

Astrophysics at the Dinner Table

There wasn't room enough for me;
as he grew louder, he filled the space.
I folded in on myself—so small, so quiet—
no one could find me; not even myself.

He filled the space, growing louder.
The shadows cowered in the corners.
No one could find me, I'd lost myself
hiding from my gentle father's rage.

The shadows sheltered in the corners—
no, that was my imagination.
They weren't hiding from my gentle father;
he was only man-sized, not a nightmare.

That was only my imagination:
anger I didn't understand, the raised voice
transformed him from man to a nightmare—
my kind father with the raging mouth.

I didn't understand the anger or the raised voice,
truth-shattering anger, spinning me with vertigo.
Now it's my husband with the raging mouth—
the one I chose; I brought him to my table.

His anger shatters my truth; I am unbalanced,
turned inside out, a collapsed star sucking light.
I brought you to my table, to my children.
Will they learn from me to shrink like shadows?

I have become a black hole, inverted;
folding in on myself, too small, too quiet.
Will my children shrink like shadows, or can they learn
to make enough room, take enough room?

You Ask Me

if I am OK.

Don't you see the movement of my chest, in and out?
And how the features on my face
mostly behave the way I ask them to?

Once I dreamed I was a butterfly
or a dolphin,
joyful and radiant—
carefree, leaping, flying—

Every morning I wake up
to the sound of your breathing beside me
knowing I will spend the day
tending to our children and our home.

This is a good arrangement
$\qquad\qquad\qquad$ for most of us.

You ask if I am OK.

Don't you see how my bones hold me up?
How my muscles pull and release?
Yes, I am

in working order.

Tightrope

It's 3 in the morning
and I've been up all night
in the nursery, with the baby,
again.

She won't sleep unless I hold her
and I've been holding her but
I can't sleep
when I'm holding her
and she won't sleep
unless I hold her.

I place her ever-so-gently into her crib
(hoping against hope)
and she cries, a sharp rebuke.
I pick her up again, sobbing,
and beg her to sleep,
but she doesn't understand me.
She doesn't understand and
she won't stop crying unless I hold her
and if I hold her I can't sleep,
and I feel the urge to shake her:
I know I have to do something.

I carry her up the stairs to our bedroom,
heart pounding, tears streaming down my face
balancing her against my exhausted body
step
       by
              step
I carry her to our bed
and shake him gently—
Please wake up.
I am so tired.
I can't do this anymore.

And he is confused
but he holds the baby for a minute,
still half-asleep.

I sit on the bed and take a breath,
a few more breaths,
my heartbeat slows.
I can do this again, I can.
He has to go to work in the morning and
he can't make mistakes at work,
he needs to be well-rested—
I know all of this,
he doesn't need to tell me again.

I take her back into my arms,
carry her, carefully,
down the stairs,
back to the nursery,
and rock her to sleep,
my tears falling on her warm body.

Where to Cry

If you cry in the shower, your sobs will be muffled by the water falling on the tiles, and the tracks of your tears will be washed away, and if your eyes are red that is easily explained by a stray drop of shampoo.

If you cry at home, while your husband is at work and your children are at school, your sorrow will fill the house. The rooms will rattle with it and the halls will be haunted with it. Your despair will creep into your children's dreams.

If you cry in the car alone, it is the safest place. You can weep and scream until your nose runs and your throat is raw.

If you cry in the car while your children are with you, play their favorite songs on the radio loudly, and cry quietly. Take a breath before answering their questions, or your breaking voice will betray you. Wear your sunglasses.

If you cry in your bed, wait until the lights are off. Turn your back to the middle of the bed. Focus on stillness. Your pillow will become damp, but your tears will be silent.

Question 41, New Patient Questionnaire

Q. 41: Have you ever experienced an unwanted sexual encounter?

Have you ever, on your first date with your first boyfriend,
    let his tongue explore your surprised
    mouth and his body press you to the ground?

Have you let him reach under your shirt because
    no one had ever wanted to before?

Have you ever, after months of saying *no*, said *yes*,
    and held your breath and clenched your fists,
    and tasted unwept tears?

Have you ever, after being left and broken hearted,
    convinced yourself that sex was all
    anyone wanted from you anyway?

Have you ever just kept giving in, so you wouldn't be alone?

Have you ever thought you healed?

But then, have you ever, in the bed where your two children
    were happily conceived, prayed: *just
    let him finish, just let him finish?*

And have you ever started drinking one more glass
    of wine to numb the self-loathing that crawled
    under your skin each time you let him ignore
    your closed eyes, closed thighs?

Have you ever?

Ophidiophobia

It lived in a drawer next to his side of the bed,
coiled in a zipped green vinyl case. He asked
if I wanted to learn how to use it.
No, I said.
I didn't say, *The power to hold death
between your index finger and your thumb
belongs to the gods.*

Before our first baby learned to crawl, we
began to baby-proof our house—
moving fragile things, medicines, cleaning supplies
to top shelves, anchoring furniture,
sticking plastic plugs into open outlets—
and he bought a gun safe
(a gun *safe*? I thought)
and moved it, still coiled
in its case, into the safe, in our bedroom closet, where
it lay in wait.

The gun moved with us from house to house—
as years passed, and our children grew—
always nesting in the safe in our bedroom closet.

One night I took too many pills,
panicked and vomited.
The next day he told me
he'd hidden the gun. As if
he'd mistaken me for Cleopatra
and hidden the asps.
Proof again that he didn't know me.

When I decided to leave him,
a divorced girlfriend told me to get the gun out of the house first;
she said she'd keep it for me.

It was easy to find the safe,
easy to guess the combination,
easy to unzip the green vinyl case,
easy to pull out the gun. But

the gun
was
loaded.

I held death in my hands, the gun
ready to strike, the unexploded bullets
gleaming like fangs.

I called a friend, ex-military. From thousands of miles away,
he gave me the gift of calm
breaths and simple steps until
the bullets fell, harmless,
to the floor.
I put them in a Ziploc bag,
zipped the gun back into its case,
tucked them into my red briefcase,
locked the empty safe,
placed it back into its hiding place.
I drove the briefcase to a parking lot,
parked next to my girlfriend, gave her
the briefcase.

Months later, before I drove away
with my car full of boxes, I returned
the snake, and its fangs, to their hiding place.

He never asked me how
the bullets left
their chamber.

The Beginning

One night we stayed up talking,
walking around campus in the dark,
telling each other our stories.
When I got cold,
he gave me his jacket—
it hung past my knees, but kept me warm
and made me soften.

He pestered me about cutting classes
and not doing my homework
but that didn't bother me—
I was surprised he seemed to care.

It wasn't more than a few months
after we gave in to the inevitable
and became more than friends
that I started doing his laundry
and typing out his homework.
I began to mold myself to fit his shape.
I let him eat my grilled cheese sandwiches:
he would take them off of my plate, bite out the middle,
and leave me the edges.

Light/Dark

Like the jaw of a boxer
throwing his first punch.
Like the jaw of a soldier
as a bullet is scraped from under his skin.
Like the jaw of a woman
pushing new life from her body.

I am none of these today.
I am sitting in a soft chair
in a quiet, sunlit room,
tea steeping next to me.

And yet,
as I take a breath,
my battle-ready jaw catches me by surprise.

I breathe slowly,
relaxing into
the softness of my chair.
Everything is fine.

Five minutes pass
and my teeth are clenched down on that invisible bit again,
straining,
unreasonable,

as I sit in my soft chair,
still and silent,
in the sunlit room.

The Weaver

The spider grasped the single silk thread in her sticky legs
desperate to hold on.

The thread was once part of a web—the spider's life's work of a web—strong
and beautiful, securely anchored.

The spider still remembered every millimeter of that web intimately:
how it fit together; her favorite hiding places; where she'd patched it; where
the sun first shone through it in the morning; where the rain collected during
a storm.

Now there was just this one thread left,
and the spider clinging to it, swinging unsteadily,
as birds passed over,
hungry and watchful.

Fargo, November

Wind pulls the breath from my wool-wrapped mouth,
beats and batters against my coat,
a body bag I've zipped myself into.

Thick boots smother my feet, as
snow swallows each hard-fought step—
pull up, push down, pull up, push down.

Cold stings my exposed eyes.
Tears freeze against my face,
cementing scarf to skin.

Endless white slips into darkness
as I trudge towards the vanishing point.
Streetlights whimper into the screaming cold.

I sink deeper with each step,
as the soft snow whispers promises of repose.
The wind, a siren, sings for my surrender.

What if I just stopped

and rested here?

Soon I would be

invisible.

My Private Music

I walk without my skin—not just naked
but exposed, transparent. Blood pushing through my veins,
open to the air, moving with my heart's rhythm,
my own private music sung for strangers.

Unprotected, transparent, as the blood rushes through my veins.
What is bravery if not walking without skin?
Strangers listen to my private music, watching
my muscles expand, contract, my synapses spark.

This is bravery: walking without skin,
taking one more step with un-soled feet,
muscles expanding and contracting, synapses sparking,
living life forward, getting out of bed each morning.

Each step overwhelms my un-soled feet;
what hurts is not the pebbles or the blades of grass,
or getting out of bed every morning, but
the sneer on my beloved's face.

The grass spears my feet, a small agony compared
to barbed words flung from my father's mouth,
the contempt in my lover's voice—
my trust met with a thousand cuts.

My mother hurled spined words
that wormed their way through my defenses.
A thousand cuts in return for my trust,
my imperfections laid bare, scrutinized.

I am defenseless, worn down,
my beating heart broken open to the air,
every fault dissected, pored over
but I take another step without my skin.

The Night Before My Husband Hid the Gun

I sent him a late afternoon text message so I'd know when to have dinner ready. He responded: *I'm not coming home. You said you don't love me anymore.* I looked at our two children, busy with coloring books and crayons at the kitchen table, and took another sip of wine. *You have to come home. What will I tell them?* I began to prepare dinner for three, still sipping my glass of boxed red wine. I tried again: *We'll talk about it. Please come home.* I didn't say, "maybe I still love you" or "this isn't the end." He came home, hugged the kids, retreated to the basement. I started on a second glass as fear clutched in my stomach. I helped brush teeth, pulled nightgowns over small heads, read bedtime stories. Said "good night," and "I love you," kissed foreheads, went to the kitchen and filled another glass.

Before that night I'd always hidden my hurtful truths, carried them with me until they grew too heavy. I hadn't meant to let that truth escape, but I had lost the strength to hold them all in.

He texted me from the basement: *What did I do? Why don't you love me anymore?* The answer was he hadn't done anything without my permission. I'd let him break my heart so slowly, given pieces of myself for years, quieted my voice until I forgot what it sounded like, believed that what was left was all that I deserved. So when depression settled into my bones, neither of us understood why. The answer was I had no heart left to love him.

Another glass of wine. My vision was blurring, but I still saw myself too clearly—cruel, weak, selfish—when my whole life I'd tried to be kind, strong, generous. Unable to reconcile with myself, I stumbled upstairs, shook the bottle of trazadone pills into my open palm, and washed them down with wine.

One minute later, it hit me.

I texted him to tell him what I'd done. *Make yourself puke,* he texted back. *Drink a lot of water.* I stared through wet eyes at the bitter ruby liquid in the toilet, made myself throw up again, tears and vomit spilling out of me. I drank a glass of water, and another, desperate for absolution, and crawled into bed.

The next thing I remember: waking up, head splitting, feeling his weight in bed next to me,

too heavy.

Flight

Perched at the open hinged door, just outside of the filigreed golden wires, she cocks her head to look back inside.

Seeds and plump pieces of fruit are scattered on the cage floor. She pauses, considering, when her gaze falls on the golden swing, suspended and riderless, and iron squeezes her fluttering heart.

She steadies herself, and turns to look at the world beyond. She does not know what dangers lurk there or what wonders may reveal themselves. She does not see any seeds or fruit, or any golden swings.

The air flows differently around her body here, outside the cage. It whispers freedom to her feathers and sings joy to her heart. Her pulse quickens.

She knows what is behind her, and that this door will not always be open.

One last look back, and then

she lifts her wings

and flies into the unknown.

The Big Red Grill

He spent months researching
grills—the red one and
the green one—weighing
pros, cons, reviews, specifications,
features, sizes, grilling times, and spent hours
telling me everything
he'd learned and asking
for my opinion so he could ignore it.

Meanwhile, I moved through life
ten seconds at a time because ten
seconds was all I could manage—
ten seconds, and another ten
seconds, and days that wouldn't
end, and sleep that wouldn't
come, and dark that wouldn't dissipate
because it was trapped inside
my skin, behind
my eyes.

He assured the grill salesman who didn't
do deliveries that someone would be home
to help unload the big red grill. So when I opened
the door to the gray-haired older man,
he looked me up and down and said
he would come back when my husband
was home. He didn't know how many burdens
I had already carried for my husband.
I reassured him: I was strong (in some ways).

And so—down the snowy sidewalk, up
the icy stairs, the old man and I
pushed that 372-pound grill, slipping, gripping,
grunting, as the wind whistled
and fought against us, until the grill
landed in its place of honor
on the deck. The man shook my
hand, shook his head, and left.

My ex took the big red grill
with him to his new home.
I wonder if his new wife
had to move it into place. Every
time I drop our children off
there, I see that grill—a monument to what I carried,
and what I left behind.

My (Un)Broken Home

Before I broke my home,
here is what I had become:
      arms for rocking
      breasts for feeding
      eyes to watch for unseen dangers
      ears to hear midnight cries
      mouth for singing lullabies
      hands for washing, folding, cooking
      legs for running after children

Before I broke my home,
here is what my children learned:
      a mother is arms, breasts, eyes, ears, mouth, hands, legs,
      without a self, a spirit
while
      a father smiles and nods,
      accepting the bargain
she has made.

For My Younger Child

> *I wasn't there, but this is how I imagine it:*

You're poised on the edge of the living room couch
with your brother, feet swinging, called away from your
cartoons. Through the window, gray melting
snow is draped across the back yard.

> *Weeks ago, I'd filled bowls of fresh fallen
> snow for both of you, mixed it with
> sugar and milk and vanilla, sweet
> and crisp on your tongue.*

On the couch, your brother waits, trembling,
like the grass in the thawing dirt.
Your dad, who never cries, is sobbing,
holding your left hand in his right,
your brother's right hand in his left.
"Kids," he says, his voice breaking across
your bones, "your mom is leaving me."

> *I was on my way home, a delayed flight
> from Chicago. I'd begged your dad to wait
> so we could talk to you both together, reassure
> you, tell you how loved you were, that
> this wasn't your fault, but—*

He takes another breath, tears melting down his cheeks.
"She doesn't love me anymore," he says.
This makes even less sense to you. You look up at your brother;
he is shaking like leaves in the Fargo wind.

> *For months your brother told me he felt something terrible
> coming, and I'd lied to soothe his fears
> and mine, living in disbelief a little while longer.*

Then you hear the words cracking in your dad's mouth—
his sadness like the ice-covered lake behind your house,
deep and treacherous.
You look at your hand swallowed up in his, squeezed too tightly.
You will not be the one to let go.

I Am the Hero In My Story and the Villain In His

I am the one who contorted myself to fit him,
the one who scraped my own rough places to smooth his path,
who stretched my limbs almost to breaking to bridge the gaps,
the one who hushed my voice to amplify his

I am the one who broke

I am the one who broke
him

I am the one who broke
free

I am the one who ripped us
apart to put myself back together

I am the villain in his story
and the hero in mine.

Kintsugi: A Family Portrait

Kintsugi is a Japanese art of mending pottery with lacquer mixed with gold or silver.

Now they only visit me in dreams,
although they used to be my family—
my ex-husband's kind sailor-mouthed mother
who healed many of my broken
places, loved me like her own child,
and the man who towered over me, his father.

I never lost my fear of his father,
although he was mostly kind (except in my dreams):
he made me feel like a child—
I was the quietest, the smallest in the family.
When I spoke to him, my voice quavered, broke,
though I knew he bore scars from his own mother.

Maybe I felt a kinship in his unhealed scars, my mother
once smashed a vase, a gift from my father.
This is what my sister and I learned: parents' broken
edges shred their children's wings, unfulfilled dreams
fester in our parents, wounded by their own families.
Sometimes I cry over the girl I was, the scared child

who didn't know what it meant to be a child,
who devoted herself to placating a volatile mother,
the child who held her breath, hid her voice, for her family,
to stave off rare eruptions from her father.
Demons, witches, and silent screams filled her dreams—
but I didn't know that I was broken.

Decades later, I found my voice, used it to break
my marriage, to shatter the ground beneath my children,
to unsettle their days, fracture their dreams.
They knew their home was broken by their mother,
that I brought the tears streaking the face of their father.
How could they understand why I ripped apart their family?

Now, years later, my children have two families,
parents and stepparents, two homes unbroken.
His parents don't speak to me; his father
ignores me, the mother of his favorite grandchild.
The woman who mothered me more than my own mother
now speaks to me with rebuke and rage, and only in my dreams.

But I mend my family's fractures with the most beautiful dreams,
dreams for my children (still wounded by their father)
solid and certain in their mother's love, healing what was broken.

How to Escape a Burning House

Step 1: Notice that your house is on fire. Perhaps the smoke alarm just started beeping. Or it's been beeping for years, and the sound suddenly slipped into your consciousness. Or you were asleep and jolted awake by the smell of smoke or the flames licking your toes.

Step 2: Find the source. Look for wisps of smoke curling from your eyes after you've cried all your tears; hear the flames crackle in the words that filled your ears; smell the cinders of burnt hopes swirling through your nostrils; taste the acrid retorts you've trapped in your mouth; feel the acid roiling in your stomach. *Your* eyes, *your* ears, *your* nostrils, *your* mouth, *your* stomach: you are the fire, and now the kindling you've stacked so carefully has caught.

Step 3. Burn the building. You. Are. Burning. This house has lost its claim on you. There is only one thing you can do: burn it down.

Step 4. Become a torch. You-as-fire light the way for other captives— the ones who don't hear their own smoke alarms, the ones still hiding their kindling from themselves. Your flames call to them, their kindling catches and they begin to burn.

Step 5. Rise. As the flames die down, you brush off the ashes and unfurl your wings. It is time to soar.

Reunion

My old companions,
Despair, Anxiety, and Resentment,
are setting up shop again,
drawing all of the curtains to darken my mood,
bringing the teapot to an insistent scream of a boil,
sharpening nails to dig ever so slightly into my skin.

I can't just wish them away
or hope that they'll feel unwelcome and leave.

So first I greet them:
Hello, Despair.
Good morning, Anxiety.
Hi, Resentment.

And then I look at each of them.
(Without Despair, I wouldn't have had the courage to climb the mountain.
Without Anxiety, I wouldn't have known that it was time to break through my chrysalis.
Without Resentment, I wouldn't have learned how sweet life is.)
So I look at each of them
and thank them.

As they turn to leave,
I tell them goodbye,
knowing I'll see them again,
the next time I need to remember
why they were my companions.

I Know This Is a Bad Time

All the times are bad right now: you're doing laundry washing
dishes making dinner reading bedtime stories checking homework
calming tantrums wiping tears shopping for groceries changing
diapers bathing small bodies making lunches scheduling doctor's
appointments and summer camps and playdates

Your life is an infinite to-do list, and
joy is a song you've forgotten how to sing.

Listen to me:
        you deserve so much more.

You will have to fight for it, and it will feel like the hardest thing
you've ever done, but—don't you see?—
you are already living the hardest life right now.

Listen:
        you are ready,

your joy is waiting for you.

The Playground

play with me

my eyes reflect
the light in these two small smiling faces

hide and seek
tag you're it and run
slide, swing, jump, spin
live any story you imagine

we shriek,
zipping down slides,
swinging so high our feet touch the sky

        I

                jump

knowing I might fall, but
my children see the joy in me

chasing villains with laser swords
we eat our 10-scoop ice cream cones
and ride on unicorns

once we've won the battle
we come back for seconds
with sprinkles and whipped cream
cost: two kisses each

I find my balance on the high stone wall
forget to tuck my windblown hair
behind my ears

we tumble down hills
make mudpies
smudge our rumpled clothes

my voice used to be a whisper
        now sometimes it is a

shout!

my laughter has loosened
my heart is healing

play with me

Postmortem

It wasn't blunt force trauma,
        a heart attack, or
                a stroke.

It was more like cancer,
a rapidly reproducing malignancy
crowding out

            everything else.

He didn't beat me,
      or cheat on me,
           or become an addict.

He just made me
small,
and
        so
              (quiet)

    I couldn't hear my own voice.

I was desperate not to inconvenience
him, desperate
to smooth over
every rough
edge, to
grind
myself
down,
until
there was nothing

                left.

He Felt Like Home

I loved him because he felt like home—
arms that held me tight, walls to keep me safe.

Arms that held me tight, walls to hem me in.
Home meant safety and protection.

He was safety and protection, but
safe is not secure; protection, not acceptance.

Home was not secure, home did not accept me.
I had to work for love at home, I had to hide myself.

I worked at loving him so hard I nearly lost myself—
I left him because he felt like home.

ACKNOWLEDGMENTS

An earlier version of "The Weaver" was originally published as "Tightrope" (under the author's former name) in Mutabilis Press's *Enchantment of the Ordinary*.

I owe the deepest debt of gratitude to David Meischen, who introduced me to the art of poetry, and then continued to nurture and encourage me decades later when I found my way back to poetry. This book would not have been possible without his guidance and support. I am also eternally grateful for Tina Carlson, Cindy Huyser, Radha Marcum, and Scott McDaniel for their spot-on critiques, brilliant suggestions, and rich fellowship. Several other poets have helped me refine these poems, and I'm so thankful for their insights as well: Margo Davis, Sandi Stromberg, John Milkereit, Stan Crawford, Varsha Saraiya-Shah, Gabrielle Langley, Mark Childs, Elizabeth Kropf, and Zelda Lockhart.

I am also thankful for David Lawrence, who helped me find my way back to myself and keeps reminding me who I am; and for my children, who have made all of this—and everything yet to come—worthwhile.

Eileen Lawrence began writing poetry in high school under the expert guidance of her freshman English teacher. She continued writing poetry while earning a music literature degree and a law degree. After finishing law school, Eileen devoted her writing time to legal writing—as an associate attorney for a couple of law firms, as an assistant professor, and then as an Assistant City Attorney. After the birth of her second child, Eileen left her legal career to stay home with her children and found herself turning back to poetry as a therapeutic creative outlet and survival mechanism.

Although Eileen now runs her own law firm, she has continued writing poetry and takes poetry classes from that same freshman English teacher, David Meischen. In her free time, Eileen writes about mental health and being human in her Substack newsletter, *Notes From the Mindfield*. She lives in central Texas with her husband, her two children, and their three cats, and can be found online as @eileenwritesit and at eileenwrites.net.

Eileen's poetry has been published by *Dos Gatos Press*, *Mutabilis Press*, the Fargo Public Library, *Visions International*, *Equinox Journal*, and *Kindred Characters*, and online in *The Ekphrastic Review* and *formidable woman sanctuary*.

www.ingramcontent.com/pod-product-compliance
Lightning Source LLC
Chambersburg PA
CBHW030059170426
43197CB00010B/1599